Krapp's Last Tape
and Embers

SAMUEL BECKETT

Krapp's Last Tape
and
Embers

faber and faber

First published in 1959
by Faber and Faber Limited
3 Queen Square London WC1N 3AU
First published in this edition 1965
Reset 2006

Typeset by RefineCatch Limited, Bungay, Suffolk
Printed in England by
Mackays of Chatham PLC, Chatham, Kent

Every effort has been made to contact all copyright holders of
photographs. The publisher would be pleased to rectify any omissions
or errors brought to their notice at the earliest convenience

All applications for performing rights in *Krapp's Last Tape*
and *Embers* should be addressed to:
Curtis Brown Ltd, 4th Floor, Haymarket House,
28/29 Haymarket, London SW1Y 4SP

The right of Samuel Beckett to be identified
as author of this work has been asserted in accordance
with Section 77 of the Copyright, Designs and Patents Act 1988

A CIP record for this book
is available from the British Library

ISBN 0–571–22913–1

2 4 6 8 10 9 7 5 3 1

The first performance in Great Britain of *Krapp's Last Tape* was given at the Royal Court Theatre, Sloane Square, London, on 28th October 1958. It was directed by Donald McWhinnie; and Krapp was played by Patrick Magee.

Embers, a new play specially written for broadcasting, was first performed in the B.B.C. Third Programme on 24th June 1959. The cast was as follows:

HENRY Jack MacGowran
ADA Kathleen Michael
ADDIE Kathleen Helme
THE MUSIC MASTER ⎫
and   ⎬ Patrick Magee
THE RIDING MASTER ⎭
Pianist: Cicely Hoye
Produced by Donald McWhinnie

Krapp's Last Tape

A late evening in the future.

    KRAPP's *den.*

    Front centre a small table, the two drawers of which open towards the audience.

    Sitting at the table, facing front, i.e. across from the drawers, a wearish old man: KRAPP.

    Rusty black narrow trousers too short for him. Rusty black sleeveless waistcoat, four capacious pockets. Heavy silver watch and chain. Grimy white shirt open at neck, no collar. Surprising pair of dirty white boots, size ten at least, very narrow and pointed.

    White face. Purple nose. Disordered grey hair. Unshaven.

    Very near-sighted (but unspectacled). Hard of hearing.

    Cracked voice. Distinctive intonation.

    Laborious walk.

    On the table a tape-recorder with microphone and a number of cardboard boxes containing reels of recorded tapes.

    Table and immediately adjacent area in strong white light. Rest of stage in darkness.

    KRAPP *remains a moment motionless, heaves a great sigh, looks at his watch, fumbles in his pockets, takes out an envelope, puts it back, fumbles, takes out a small bunch of keys, raises it to his eyes, chooses a key, gets up and moves to front of table. He stoops, unlocks first drawer, peers into it, feels about inside it, takes out a reel of tape, peers at it, puts it back, locks drawer, unlocks second drawer, peers into it, feels about inside it, takes out a large banana, peers at it, locks drawer, puts keys back in his pocket. He turns, advances to edge of stage, halts, strokes banana, peels it, drops skin at his feet, puts end of banana in his mouth and remains motionless, staring vacuously before him. Finally he bites off the end, turns aside and begins pacing to and fro at edge of stage, in the light,*

*i.e. not more than four or five paces either way, meditatively
eating banana. He treads on skin, slips, nearly falls, recovers himself,
stoops and peers at skin and finally pushes it, still stooping, with his
foot over edge of stage into pit. He resumes his pacing, finishes
banana, returns to table, sits down, remains a moment motionless,
heaves a great sigh, takes keys from his pockets, raises them to
his eyes, chooses key, gets up and moves to front of table, unlocks
second drawer, takes out a second large banana, peers at it, locks
drawer, puts back keys in his pocket, turns, advances to edge of
stage, halts, strokes banana, peels it, tosses skin into pit, puts end of
banana in his mouth and remains motionless, staring vacuously
before him. Finally he has an idea, puts banana in his waistcoat
pocket, the end emerging, and goes with all the speed he can muster
backstage into darkness. Ten seconds. Loud pop of cork. Fifteen
seconds. He comes back into light carrying an old ledger and sits
down at table. He lays ledger on table, wipes his mouth, wipes his
hands on the front of his waistcoat, brings them smartly together
and rubs them.*

KRAPP: (*briskly*). Ah! (*He bends over ledger, turns the pages, finds
the entry he wants, reads.*) Box . . . thrree . . . spool . . .
five. (*He raises his head and stares front. With relish.*) Spool!
(*Pause.*) Spooool! (*Happy smile. Pause. He bends over table,
starts peering and poking at the boxes.*) Box . . . thrree . . .
thrree . . . four . . . two . . . (*with surprise*) nine! good
God! . . . seven . . . ah! the little rascal! (*He takes up box,
peers at it.*) Box thrree. (*He lays it on table, opens it and
peers at spools inside.*) Spool . . . (*he peers at ledger*) . . . five
. . . (*he peers at spools*) . . . five . . . five . . . ah! the little
scoundrel! (*He takes out a spool, peers at it.*) Spool five.
(*He lays it on table, closes box three, puts it back with the
others, takes up the spool.*) Box thrree, spool five. (*He bends
over the machine, looks up. With relish.*) Spooool! (*Happy
smile. He bends, loads spool on machine, rubs his hands.*) Ah!
(*He peers at ledger, reads entry at foot of page.*) Mother at
rest at last . . . Hm. . . . The black ball. . . . (*He raises
his head, stares blankly front. Puzzled.*) Black ball? . . .

(*He peers again at ledger, reads.*) The dark nurse. . . .
(*He raises his head, broods, peers again at ledger, reads.*)
Slight improvement in bowel condition. . . . Hm. . . .
Memorable . . . what? (*He peers closer.*) Equinox,
memorable equinox. (*He raises his head, stares blankly
front. Puzzled.*) Memorable equinox? . . . (*Pause. He
shrugs his shoulders, peers again at ledger, reads.*)
Farewell to—(*he turns page*)—love.
*He raises his head, broods, bends over machine, switches on
and assumes listening posture, i.e. leaning forward, elbows
on table, hand cupping ear towards machine, face front.*

TAPE: (*strong voice, rather pompous, clearly Krapp's at a
much earlier time*). Thirty-nine today, sound as a—
(*Settling himself more comfortably he knocks one of the
boxes off the table, curses, switches off, sweeps boxes and
ledger violently to the ground, winds tape back to
beginning, switches on, resumes posture.*) Thirty-nine
today, sound as a bell, apart from my old weakness,
and intellectually I have now every reason to suspect
at the . . . (*hesitates*) . . . crest of the wave—or
thereabouts. Celebrated the awful occasion, as in
recent years, quietly at the Wine-house. Not a soul.
Sat before the fire with closed eyes, separating the
grain from the husks. Jotted down a few notes, on the
back of an envelope. Good to be back in my den, in
my old rags. Have just eaten I regret to say three
bananas and only with difficulty refrained from a
fourth. Fatal things for a man with my condition.
(*Vehemently.*) Cut 'em out! (*Pause.*) The new light
above my table is a great improvement. With all this
darkness round me I feel less alone. (*Pause.*) In a way.
(*Pause.*) I love to get up and move about in it, then
back here to . . . (*hesitates*) . . . me. (*Pause.*) Krapp.
Pause.
The grain, now what I wonder do I mean by that, I
mean . . . (*hesitates*) . . . I suppose I mean those things

worth having when all the dust has—when all *my* dust has settled. I close my eyes and try and imagine them.
Pause. KRAPP *closes his eyes briefly.*
Extraordinary silence this evening, I strain my ears and do not hear a sound. Old Miss McGlome always sings at this hour. But not tonight. Songs of her girlhood, she says. Hard to think of her as a girl. Wonderful woman though. Connaught, I fancy. (*Pause.*) Shall I sing when I am her age, if I ever am? No. (*Pause.*) Did I sing as a boy? No. (*Pause.*) Did I ever sing? No.
Pause.
Just been listening to an old year, passages at random. I did not check in the book, but it must be at least ten or twelve years ago. At that time I think I was still living on and off with Bianca in Kedar Street. Well out of that, Jesus yes! Hopeless business. (*Pause.*) Not much about her, apart from a tribute to her eyes. Very warm. I suddenly saw them again. (*Pause.*) Incomparable! (*Pause.*) Ah well. . . . (*Pause.*) These old P.M.s are gruesome, but I often find them—(KRAPP *switches off, broods, switches on*)—a help before embarking on a new . . . (*hesitates*) . . . retrospect. Hard to believe I was ever that young whelp. The voice! Jesus! And the aspirations! (*Brief laugh in which* KRAPP *joins.*) And the resolutions! (*Brief laugh in which* KRAPP *joins.*) To drink less, in particular. (*Brief laugh of* KRAPP *alone.*) Statistics. Seventeen hundred hours, out of the preceding eight thousand odd, consumed on licensed premises alone. More than 20 per cent, say 40 per cent of his waking life. (*Pause.*) Plans for a less . . . (*hesitates*) . . . engrossing sexual life. Last illness of his father. Flagging pursuit of happiness. Unattainable laxation. Sneers at what he calls his youth and thanks to God that it's over. (*Pause.*) False ring there. (*Pause.*) Shadows of the opus . . . magnum. Closing with a—(*brief laugh*)—yelp to Providence. (*Prolonged laugh in which* KRAPP *joins.*) What remains of all

that misery? A girl in a shabby green coat, on a railway-station platform? No?

Pause.

When I look—

KRAPP *switches off, broods, looks at his watch, gets up, goes backstage into darkness. Ten seconds. Pop of cork. Ten seconds. Second cork. Ten seconds. Third cork. Ten seconds. Brief burst of quavering song.*

KRAPP: (*sings*). Now the day is over,
              Night is drawing nigh-igh,
              Shadows—

Fit of coughing. He comes back into light, sits down, wipes his mouth, switches on, resumes his listening posture.

TAPE: —back on the year that is gone, with what I hope is perhaps a glint of the old eye to come, there is of course the house on the canal where mother lay a-dying, in the late autumn, after her long viduity (KRAPP *gives a start*), and the—(KRAPP *switches off, winds back tape a little, bends his ear closer to machine, switches on*)—a-dying, after her long viduity, and the—

KRAPP *switches off, raises his head, stares blankly before him. His lips move in the syllables of 'viduity'. No sound. He gets up, goes backstage into darkness, comes back with an enormous dictionary, lays it on table, sits down and looks up the word.*

KRAPP: (*reading from dictionary*). State—or condition—of being —or remaining—a widow—or widower. (*Looks up. Puzzled.*) Being—or remaining? . . . (*Pause. He peers again at dictionary. Reading.*) 'Deep weeds of viduity.' . . . Also of an animal, especially a bird . . . the vidua or weaver-bird . . . Black plumage of male. . . . (*He looks up. With relish.*) The vidua-bird!

Pause. He closes dictionary, switches on, resumes listening posture.

TAPE: —bench by the weir from where I could see her window. There I sat, in the biting wind, wishing she were

7

gone. (*Pause*.) Hardly a soul, just a few regulars,
nursemaids, infants, old men, dogs, I got to know them
quite well—oh by appearance of course I mean! One dark
young beauty I recollect particularly, all white and starch,
incomparable bosom, with a big black hooded
perambulator, most funereal thing. Whenever I looked in
her direction she had her eyes on me. And yet when I was
bold enough to speak to her—not having been
introduced—she threatened to call a policeman. As if I
had designs on her virtue! (*Laugh. Pause*.) The face she
had! The eyes! Like . . . (*hesitates*) . . . chrysolite! (*Pause*.)
Ah well. . . . (*Pause*.) I was there when—(KRAPP *switches
off, broods, switches on again*)—the blind went down, one of
those dirty brown roller affairs, throwing a ball for a little
white dog as chance would have it. I happened to look up
and there it was. All over and done with, at last. I sat on
for a few moments with the ball in my hand and the dog
yelping and pawing at me. (*Pause*.) Moments. Her
moments, my moments. (*Pause*.) The dog's moments.
(*Pause*.) In the end I held it out to him and he took it in
his mouth, gently, gently. A small, old, black, hard, solid
rubber ball. (*Pause*.) I shall feel it, in my hand, until my
dying day. (*Pause*.) I might have kept it. (*Pause*.) But I
gave it to the dog.
Pause.
Ah well. . . .
Pause.
Spiritually a year of profound gloom and indigence until
that memorable night in March, at the end of the jetty, in
the howling wind, never to be forgotten, when suddenly
I saw the whole thing. The vision at last. This I fancy is
what I have chiefly to record this evening, against the
day when my work will be done and perhaps no place
left in my memory, warm or cold, for the miracle
that . . . (*hesitates*) . . . for the fire that set it alight. What
I suddenly saw then was this, that the belief I had been

going on all my life, namely—(KRAPP *switches off impatiently, winds tape forward, switches on again*)—great granite rocks the foam flying up in the light of the lighthouse and the wind-gauge spinning like a propeller, clear to me at last that the dark I have always struggled to keep under is in reality my most—(KRAPP *curses, switches off, winds tape forward, switches on again*)—unshatterable association until my dissolution of storm and night with the light of the understanding and the fire—(KRAPP *curses louder, switches off, winds tape forward, switches on again*—my face in her breasts and my hand on her. We lay there without moving. But under us all moved, and moved us, gently, up and down, and from side to side.

Pause.

Past midnight. Never knew such silence. The earth might be uninhabited.

Pause.

Here I end—

KRAPP *switches off, winds tape back, switches on again.*—upper lake, with the punt, bathed off the bank, then pushed out into the stream and drifted. She lay stretched out on the floorboards with her hands under her head and her eyes closed. Sun blazing down, bit of a breeze, water nice and lively. I noticed a scratch on her thigh and asked her how she came by it. Picking gooseberries, she said. I said again I thought it was hopeless and no good going on and she agreed, without opening her eyes. (*Pause.*) I asked her to look at me and after a few moments—(*pause*)—after a few moments she did, but the eyes just slits, because of the glare. I bent over her to get them in the shadow and they opened. (*Pause. Low.*) Let me in. (*Pause.*) We drifted in among the flags and stuck. The way they went down, sighing, before the stem! (*Pause.*) I lay down across her with my face in her breasts and my hand on her. We lay there without moving. But under us all moved, and moved us, gently, up and down, and from side to side.

Pause.

Past midnight. Never knew—

KRAPP *switches off, broods. Finally he fumbles in his pockets, encounters the banana, takes it out, peers at it, puts it back, fumbles, brings out envelope, fumbles, puts back envelope, looks at his watch, gets up and goes backstage into darkness. Ten seconds. Sound of bottle against glass, then brief siphon. Ten seconds. Bottle against glass alone. Ten seconds. He comes back a little unsteadily into light, goes to front of table, takes out keys, raises them to his eyes, chooses key, unlocks first drawer, peers into it, feels about inside, takes out reel, peers at it, locks drawer, puts keys back in his pocket, goes and sits down, takes reel off machine, lays it on dictionary, loads virgin reel on machine, takes envelope from his pocket, consults back of it, lays it on table, switches on, clears his throat and begins to record.*

KRAPP: Just been listening to that stupid bastard I took myself for thirty years ago, hard to believe I was ever as bad as that. Thank God that's all done with anyway. (*Pause.*) The eyes she had! (*Broods, realizes he is recording silence, switches off, broods. Finally.*) Everything there, everything, all the—(*Realizes this is not being recorded, switches on.*) Everything there, everything on this old muckball, all the light and dark and famine and feasting of . . . (*hesitates*) . . . the ages! (*In a shout.*) Yes! (*Pause.*) Let that go! Jesus! Take his mind off his homework! Jesus! (*Pause. Weary.*) Ah well, maybe he was right. (*Pause.*) Maybe he was right. (*Broods. Realizes. Switches off. Consults envelope.*) Pah! (*Crumples it and throws it away. Broods. Switches on.*) Nothing to say, not a squeak. What's a year now? The sour cud and the iron stool. (*Pause.*) Revelled in the word spool. (*With relish.*) Spoooool! Happiest moment of the past half million. (*Pause.*) Seventeen copies sold, of which eleven at trade price to free circulating libraries beyond

the seas. Getting known. (*Pause.*) One pound six and
something, eight I have little doubt. (*Pause.*) Crawled out
once or twice, before the summer was cold. Sat shivering
in the park, drowned in dreams and burning to be gone.
Not a soul. (*Pause.*) Last fancies. (*Vehemently.*) Keep 'em
under! (*Pause.*) Scalded the eyes out of me reading *Effie*
again, a page a day, with tears again. Effie. . . . (*Pause.*)
Could have been happy with her, up there on the Baltic,
and the pines, and the dunes. (*Pause.*) Could I? (*Pause.*)
And she? (*Pause.*) Pah! (*Pause.*) Fanny came in a couple of
times. Bony old ghost of a whore. Couldn't do much, but
I suppose better than a kick in the crutch. The last time
wasn't so bad. How do you manage it, she said, at your
age? I told her I'd been saving up for her all my life.
(*Pause.*) Went to Vespers once, like when I was in short
trousers. (*Pause. Sings.*)

> Now the day is over,
> Night is drawing nigh-igh,
> Shadows—(*coughing, then almost inaudible*)—
>   of the evening
> Steal across the sky.

(*Gasping.*) Went to sleep and fell off the pew. (*Pause.*)
Sometimes wondered in the night if a last effort mightn't—
(*Pause.*) Ah finish your booze now and get to your bed. Go
on with this drivel in the morning. Or leave it at that.
(*Pause.*) Leave it at that. (*Pause.*) Lie propped up in the
dark—and wander. Be again in the dingle on a Christmas
Eve, gathering holly, the red-berried. (*Pause.*) Be again on
Croghan on a Sunday morning, in the haze, with the bitch,
stop and listen to the bells. (*Pause.*) And so on. (*Pause.*) Be
again, be again. (*Pause.*) All that old misery. (*Pause.*) Once
wasn't enough for you. (*Pause.*) Lie down across her.
*Long pause. He suddenly bends over machine, switches off,
wrenches off tape, throws it away, puts on the other, winds it
forward to the passage he wants, switches on, listens staring
front.*

TAPE: —gooseberries, she said. I said again I thought it was hopeless and no good going on and she agreed, without opening her eyes. (*Pause.*) I asked her to look at me and after a few moments—(*Pause*)—after a few moments she did, but the eyes just slits, because of the glare. I bent over her to get them in the shadow and they opened. (*Pause. Low.*) Let me in. (*Pause.*) We drifted in among the flags and stuck. The way they went down, sighing, before the stem! (*Pause.*) I lay down across her with my face in her breasts and my hand on her. We lay there without moving. But under us all moved, and moved us, gently, up and down, and from side to side.

Pause. KRAPP's *lips move. No sound.*

Past midnight. Never knew such silence. The earth might be uninhabited.

Pause.

Here I end this reel. Box—(*pause*)—three, spool—(*pause*)—five. (*Pause.*) Perhaps my best years are gone. When there was a chance of happiness. But I wouldn't want them back. Not with the fire in me now. No, I wouldn't want them back.

KRAPP *motionless staring before him. The tape runs on in silence.*

CURTAIN

Embers

Sea scarcely audible.
HENRY*'s boots on shingle. He halts.*
Sea a little louder.

HENRY: On. (*Sea. Voice louder.*) On! (*He moves on. Boots on
shingle. As he goes.*) Stop. (*Boots on shingle. As he goes,
louder.*) Stop! (*He halts. Sea a little louder.*) Down. (*Sea.
Voice louder.*) Down! (*Slither of shingle as he sits. Sea, still
faint, audible throughout what follows whenever pause
indicated.*) (Who is beside me now? (*Pause.*) An old man,
blind and foolish. (*Pause.*) My father, back from the
dead, to be with me. (*Pause.*) As if he hadn't died.
(*Pause.*) No, simply back from the dead, to be with me,
in this strange place. (*Pause.*) Can he hear me? (*Pause.*)
Yes, he must hear me. (*Pause.*) To answer me? (*Pause.*)
No, he doesn't answer me. (*Pause.*) Just be with me.
(*Pause.*) That sound you hear is the sea. (*Pause. Louder.*)
I say that sound you hear is the sea, we are sitting on the
strand. (*Pause.*) I mention it because the sound is so
strange, so unlike the sound of the sea, that if you didn't
see what it was you wouldn't know what it was. (*Pause.*)
Hooves! (*Pause. Louder.*) Hooves! (*Sound of hooves
walking on hard road. They die rapidly away. Pause.*) Again!
(*Hooves as before. Pause. Excitedly.*) Train it to mark time!
Shoe it with steel and tie it up in the yard, have it stamp
all day! (*Pause.*) A ten-ton mammoth back from the
dead, shoe it with steel and have it tramp the world
down! (*Pause.*) Listen to it! (*Pause.*) Listen to the light
now, you always loved light, not long past noon and all
the shore in shadow and the sea out as far as the island.
(*Pause.*) You would never live this side of the bay, you

wanted the sun on the water for that evening bathe you took once too often. But when I got your money I moved across, as perhaps you may know. (*Pause.*) We never found your body, you know, that held up probate an unconscionable time, they said there was nothing to prove you hadn't run away from us all and alive and well under a false name in the Argentine for example, that grieved mother greatly. (*Pause.*) I'm like you in that, can't stay away from it, but I never go in, no, I think the last time I went in was with you. (*Pause.*) Just be near it. (*Pause.*) Today it's calm, but I often hear it above in the house and walking the roads and start talking, oh just loud enough to drown it, nobody notices. (*Pause.*) But I'd be talking now no matter where I was, I once went to Switzerland to get away from the cursed thing and never stopped all the time I was there. (*Pause.*) I usen't to need anyone, just to myself, stories, there was a great one about an old fellow called Bolton, I never finished it, I never finished any of them, I never finished anything, everything always went on for ever. (*Pause.*) Bolton. (*Pause. Louder.*) Bolton! (*Pause.*) There before the fire. (*Pause.*) Before the fire with all the shutters . . . no, hangings, hangings, all the hangings drawn and the light, no light, only the light of the fire, sitting there in the . . . no, standing, standing there on the hearthrug in the dark before the fire with his arms on the chimney-piece and his head on his arms, standing there waiting in the dark before the fire in his old red dressing-gown and no sound in the house of any kind, only the sound of the fire. (*Pause.*) Standing there in his old red dressing-gown might go on fire any minute like when he was a child, no, that was his pyjamas, standing there waiting in the dark, no light, only the light of the fire, and no sound of any kind, only the fire, an old man in great trouble. (*Pause.*) Ring then at the door and over he goes to the window and looks out between the hangings, fine old chap, very big and strong, bright winter's night, snow everywhere, bitter cold, white world, cedar boughs bending under load, and then as the arm goes up to ring again recognizes . . . Holloway . . . (*long pause*) . . . yes, Holloway, recognizes Holloway, goes down and opens. (*Pause.*) Outside all still, not a sound, dog's chain maybe or a bough groaning if you stood there listening long enough, white world, Holloway with his little black bag, not a sound, bitter cold, full moon small and white, crooked trail of Holloway's galoshes, Vega in the Lyre very green. (*Pause.*) Vega in the Lyre very green. (*Pause.*) Following conversation then on the step, no, in the room, back in the room, following conversation then back in the room, Holloway: 'My dear Bolton, it is now past midnight, if you would be good enough—', gets no further, Bolton: 'Please! PLEASE!' Dead silence then, not a sound, only the fire, all coal, burning down now, Holloway on the hearthrug trying to toast his arse, Bolton, where's Bolton, no light, only the fire, Bolton at the window, his back to the hangings, holding them a little apart with his hand, looking out, white world, even the spire, white to the vane, most unusual, silence in the house, not a sound, only the fire, no flames now, embers. (*Pause.*) Embers. (*Pause.*) Shifting, lapsing, furtive like, dreadful sound, Holloway on the rug, fine old chap, six foot, burly, legs apart, hands behind his back holding up the tails of his old macfarlane, Bolton at the window, grand old figure in his old red dressing-gown, back against the hangings, hand stretched out widening the chink, looking out, white world, great trouble, not a sound, only the embers, sound of dying, dying glow, Holloway, Bolton, Bolton, Holloway, old men, great trouble, white world, not a sound. (*Pause.*) Listen to it! (*Pause.*) Close your eyes and listen to it, what would you think it was? (*Pause. Vehement.*) A drip! A drip! (*Sound of drip, rapidly amplified, suddenly cut off.*) Again! (*Drip again. Amplification begins.*) No! (*Drip cut off. Pause.*) Father! (*Pause. Agitated.*) Stories,

stories, years and years of stories, till the need came on
me, for someone, to be with me, anyone, a stranger, to
talk to, imagine he hears me, years of that, and then,
now, for someone who . . . knew me, in the old days,
anyone, to be with me, imagine he hears me, what I am,
now. (*Pause.*) No good either. (*Pause.*) Not there either.
(*Pause.*) Try again. (*Pause.*) White world, not a sound.
(*Pause.*) Holloway. (*Pause.*) Holloway says he'll go,
damned if he'll sit up all night before a black grate,
doesn't understand, call a man out, an old friend, in the
cold and dark, an old friend, urgent need, bring the bag,
then not a word, no explanation, no heat, no light,
Bolton: 'Please! PLEASE!' Holloway, no refreshment, no
welcome, chilled to the medulla, catch his death, can't
understand, strange treatment, old friend, says he'll go,
doesn't move, not a sound, fire dying, white beam from
window, ghastly scene, wishes to God he hadn't come, no
good, fire out, bitter cold, great trouble, white world, not
a sound, no good. (*Pause.*) No good. (*Pause.*) Can't do it.
(*Pause.*) Listen to it! (*Pause.*) Father! (*Pause.*) You
wouldn't know me now, you'd be sorry you ever had me,
but you were that already, a washout, that's the last I
heard from you, a washout. (*Pause. Imitating father's
voice.*) 'Are you coming for a dip?' 'Come on, come on.'
'No.' Glare, stump to door, turn, glare. 'A washout, that's
all you are, a washout!' (*Violent slam of door. Pause.*)
Again! (*Slam. Pause.*) Slam life shut like that! (*Pause.*)
Washout. (*Pause.*) Wish to Christ she had. (*Pause.*) Never
met Ada, did you, or did you, I can't remember, no
matter, no one'd know her now. (*Pause.*) What turned her
against me do you think, the child I suppose, horrid little
creature, wish to God we'd never had her, I use to walk
with her in the fields, Jesus that was awful, she wouldn't
let go my hand and I mad to talk. 'Run along now,
Addie, and look at the lambs.' (*Imitating* ADDIE*'s voice.*)
'No papa.' 'Go on now, go on.' (*Plaintive.*) 'No papa.'

(*Violent.*) 'Go on with you when you're told and look at the lambs!' (ADDIE *'s loud wail. Pause.*) Ada too, conversation with her, that was something, that's what hell will be like, small chat to the babbling of Lethe about the good old days when we wished we were dead. (*Pause.*) Price of margarine fifty years ago. (*Pause.*) And now. (*Pause. With solemn indignation.*) Price of blueband now! (*Pause.*) Father! (*Pause.*) Tired of talking to you. (*Pause.*) That was always the way, walk all over the mountains with you talking and talking and then suddenly mum and home in misery and not a word to a soul for weeks, sulky little bastard, better off dead, better off dead. (*Long pause.*) Ada. (*Pause. Louder.*) Ada!

ADA: (*low remote voice throughout*). Yes.

HENRY: Have you been there long?

ADA: Some little time. (*Pause.*) Why do you stop, don't mind me. (*Pause.*) Do you want me to go away? (*Pause.*) Where is Addie?
       Pause.

HENRY: With her music master. (*Pause.*) Are you going to answer me today?

ADA: You shouldn't be sitting on the cold stones, they're bad for your growths. Raise yourself up till I slip my shawl under you. (*Pause.*) Is that better?

HENRY: No comparison, no comparison. (*Pause.*) Are you going to sit down beside me?

ADA: Yes. (*No sound as she sits.*) Like that? (*Pause.*) Or do you prefer like that? (*Pause.*) You don't care. (*Pause.*) Chilly enough I imagine, I hope you put on your jaegers. (*Pause.*) Did you put on your jaegers, Henry?

HENRY: What happened was this, I put them on and then I took them off again and then I put them on again and then I took them off again and then I put them on again and then I—

ADA: Have you them on now?

HENRY: I don't know. (*Pause.*) Hooves! (*Pause. Louder.*)

Hooves! (*Sound of hooves walking on hard road. They die rapidly away.*) Again!

Hooves as before. Pause.

ADA: Did you hear them?

HENRY: Not well.

ADA: Galloping?

HENRY: No. (*Pause.*) Could a horse mark time?

Pause.

ADA: I'm not sure that I know what you mean.

HENRY: (*irritably*). Could a horse be trained to stand still and mark time with its four legs?

ADA: Oh. (*Pause.*) The ones I used to fancy all did. (*She laughs. Pause.*) Laugh, Henry, it's not every day I crack a joke. (*Pause.*) Laugh, Henry do that for me.

HENRY: You wish *me* to laugh?

ADA: You laughed so charmingly once, I think that's what first attracted me to you. That and your smile. (*Pause.*) Come on, it will be like old times.

Pause. He tries to laugh, fails.

HENRY: Perhaps I should begin with the smile. (*Pause for smile.*) Did that attract you? (*Pause.*) Now I'll try again. (*Long horrible laugh.*) Any of the old charm there?

ADA: Oh Henry!

Pause.

HENRY: Listen to it! (*Pause.*) Lips and claws! (*Pause.*) Get away from it! Where it couldn't get at me! The Pampas! What?

ADA: Calm yourself.

HENRY: And I live on the brink of it! Why? Professional obligations? (*Brief laugh.*) Reasons of health? (*Brief laugh.*) Family ties? (*Brief laugh.*) A woman? (*Laugh in which she joins.*) Some old grave I cannot tear myself away from? (*Pause.*) Listen to it! What is it like?

ADA: It is like an old sound I used to hear. (*Pause.*) It is like another time, in the same place. (*Pause.*) It was rough, the spray came flying over us. (*Pause.*) Strange it should have

been rough then. (*Pause.*) And calm now.
Pause.

HENRY: Let us get up and go.

ADA: Go? Where? And Addie? She would be very distressed if she came and found you had gone without her. (*Pause.*) What do you suppose is keeping her?
Smart blow of cylindrical ruler on piano case. Unsteadily, ascending and descending, ADDIE *plays scale of A Flat Major, hands first together, then reversed. Pause.*

MUSIC MASTER: (*Italian accent*): Santa Cecilia!
Pause.

ADDIE: Will I play my piece now please?
Pause. MUSIC MASTER *beats two bars of waltz time with ruler on piano case.* ADDIE *plays opening bars of Chopin's 5th Waltz in A Flat Major,* MUSIC MASTER *beating time lightly with ruler as she plays. In first chord of bass, bar 5, she plays E instead of F. Resounding blow of ruler on piano case.* ADDIE *stops playing.*

MUSIC MASTER: (*violently*). Fa!

ADDIE: (*tearfully*). What?

MUSIC MASTER: (*violently*). Eff! Eff!

ADDIE: (*tearfully*). Where?

MUSIC MASTER: (*violently*). Qua! (*He thumps note.*) Fa!
Pause. ADDIE *begins again,* MUSIC MASTER *beating time lightly with ruler. When she comes to bar 5 she makes same mistake. Tremendous blow of ruler on piano case.* ADDIE *stops playing, begins to wail.*

MUSIC MASTER: (*frenziedly*). Eff! Eff! (*He hammers note.*) Eff! (*He hammers note.*) Eff!
Hammered note, "Eff!" and ADDIE*'s wail amplified to paroxysm, then suddenly cut off. Pause.*

ADA: You are silent today.

HENRY: It was not enough to drag her into the world, now she must play the piano.

ADA: She must learn. She shall learn. That—and riding.
Hooves walking.

RIDING MASTER: Now Miss! Elbows in Miss! Hands down
Miss! (*Hooves trotting.*) Now Miss! Back straight Miss!
Knees in Miss! (*Hooves cantering.*) Now Miss! Tummy in
Miss! Chin up Miss! (*Hooves galloping.*) Now Miss! Eyes
front Miss! (ADDIE *begins to wail.*) Now Miss! Now Miss!
Galloping hooves, "Now Miss!" and ADDIE'*s wail amplified to
paroxysm, then suddenly cut off. Pause.*

ADA: What are you thinking of? (*Pause.*) I was never taught,
until it was too late. All my life I regretted it.

HENRY: What was your strong point, I forget.

ADA: Oh . . . geometry I suppose, plane and solid. (*Pause.*)
First plane, then solid. (*Shingle as he gets up.*) Why do you
get up?

HENRY: I thought I might try and get as far as the water's
edge. (*Pause. With a sigh.*) And back. (*Pause.*) Stretch my
old bones.
Pause.

ADA: Well, why don't you? (*Pause.*) Don't stand there thinking
about it. (*Pause.*) Don't stand there staring. (*Pause. He goes
towards sea. Boots on shingle, say ten steps. He halts at water's
edge. Pause. Sea a little louder. Distant.*) Don't wet your
good boots.
Pause.

HENRY: Don't, don't. . . .
Sea suddenly rough.

ADA: (*twenty years earlier, imploring*). Don't! Don't!

HENRY: (*do.*   *urgent*). Darling!

ADA: (*do.*   *more feebly*). Don't!

HENRY: (*twenty years earlier, exultantly*). Darling!
Rough sea. ADA *cries out. Cry and sea amplified, cut off. End
of evocation. Pause. Sea calm. He goes back up deeply shelving
beach. Boots laborious on shingle. He halts. Pause. He moves
on. He halts. Pause. Sea calm and faint.*

ADA: Don't stand there gaping. Sit down. (*Pause. Shingle as he
sits.*) On the shawl. (*Pause.*) Are you afraid we might
touch? (*Pause.*) Henry.

HENRY: Yes.

ADA: You should see a doctor about your talking, it's worse, what must it be like for Addie? (*Pause.*) Do you know what she said to me once, when she was still quite small, she said, Mummy, why does Daddy keep on talking all the time? She heard you in the lavatory. I didn't know what to answer.

HENRY: Daddy! Addie! (*Pause.*) I told you to tell her I was praying. (*Pause.*) Roaring prayers at God and his saints.

ADA: It's very bad for the child. (*Pause.*) It's silly to say it keeps you from hearing it, it doesn't keep you from hearing it and even if it does you shouldn't be hearing it, there must be something wrong with your brain.
Pause.

HENRY: That! I shouldn't be hearing that!

ADA: I don't think you are hearing it. And if you are what's wrong with it, it's a lovely peaceful gentle soothing sound, why do you hate it? (*Pause.*) And if you hate it why don't you keep away from it? Why are you always coming down here? (*Pause.*) There's something wrong with your brain, you ought to see Holloway, he's alive still, isn't he?
Pause.

HENRY: (*wildly*). Thuds, I want thuds! Like this! (*He fumbles in the shingle, catches up two big stones and starts dashing them together.*) Stone! (*Clash.*) Stone! (*Clash.* "*Stone!*" *and clash amplified, cut off. Pause. He throws one stone away. Sound of its fall.*) That's life! (*He throws the other stone away. Sound of its fall.*) Not this . . . (*pause*) . . . sucking!

ADA: And why life? (*Pause.*) Why life, Henry? (*Pause.*) Is there anyone about?

HENRY: Not a living soul.

ADA: I thought as much. (*Pause.*) When we longed to have it to ourselves there was always someone. Now that it does not matter the place is deserted.

HENRY: Yes, you were always very sensitive to being seen in gallant conversation. The least feather of smoke on the

horizon and you adjusted your dress and became
immersed in the *Manchester Guardian*. (*Pause.*) The hole is
still there, after all these years. (*Pause. Louder.*) The hole is
still there.

ADA: What hole? The earth is full of holes.

HENRY: Where we did it at last for the first time.

ADA: Ah yes, I think I remember. (*Pause.*) The place has not
changed.

HENRY: Oh yes it has, *I* can see it. (*Confidentially.*) There is a
levelling going on! (*Pause.*) What age is she now?

ADA: I have lost count of time.

HENRY: Twelve? Thirteen? (*Pause.*) Fourteen?

ADA: I really could not tell you, Henry.

HENRY: It took us a long time to have her. (*Pause.*) Years we
kept hammering away at it. (*Pause.*) But we did it in the
end. (*Pause. Sigh.*) We had her in the end. (*Pause.*) Listen to
it! (*Pause.*) It's not so bad when you get out on it. (*Pause.*)
Perhaps I should have gone into the merchant navy.

ADA: It's only on the surface, you know. Underneath all is as
quiet as the grave. Not a sound. All day, all night, not a
sound.
Pause.

HENRY: Now I walk about with the gramophone. But I forgot
it today.

ADA: There is no sense in that. (*Pause.*) There is no sense in
trying to drown it. (*Pause.*) See Holloway.
Pause.

HENRY: Let us go for a row.

ADA: A row? And Addie? She would be very distressed if she
came and found you had gone for a row without her.
(*Pause.*) Who were you with just now? (*Pause.*) Before you
spoke to me.

HENRY: I was trying to be with my father.

ADA: Oh. (*Pause.*) No difficulty about that.

HENRY: I mean I was trying to get him to be with me. (*Pause.*)
You seem a little cruder than usual today, Ada. (*Pause.*)

I was asking him if he had ever met you, I couldn't
remember.

ADA: Well?

HENRY: He doesn't answer any more.

ADA: I suppose you have worn him out. (*Pause.*) You wore
him out living and now you are wearing him out dead.
(*Pause.*) The time comes when one cannot speak to you
any more. (*Pause.*) The time will come when no one will
speak to you at all, not even complete strangers. (*Pause.*)
You will be quite alone with your voice, there will be no
other voice in the world but yours. (*Pause.*) Do you hear
me?
Pause.

HENRY: I can't remember if he met you.

ADA: You know he met me.

HENRY: No, Ada, I don't know, I'm sorry, I have forgotten
almost everything connected with you.

ADA: You weren't there. Just your mother and sister. I had
called to fetch you, as arranged. We were to go bathing
together.
Pause.

HENRY: (*irritably*). Drive on, drive on! Why do people always
stop in the middle of what they are saying?

ADA: None of them knew where you were. Your bed had not
been slept in. They were all shouting at one another. Your
sister said she would throw herself off the cliff. Your father
got up and went out, slamming the door. I left soon
afterwards and passed him on the road. He did not see
me. He was sitting on a rock looking out to sea. I never
forgot his posture. And yet it was a common one. You
used to have it sometimes. Perhaps just the stillness, as if
he had been turned to stone. I could never make it out.
Pause.

HENRY: Keep on, keep on! (*Imploringly.*) Keep it going, Ada,
every syllable is a second gained.

ADA: That's all, I'm afraid. (*Pause.*) Go on now with your

SAMUEL BECKETT

father or your stories or whatever you were doing, don't
mind me any more.

HENRY: I can't! (*Pause.*) I can't do it any more!

ADA: You were doing it a moment ago, before you spoke to
me.

HENRY: (*angrily*). I can't do it any more now! (*Pause.*) Christ!
Pause.

ADA: Yes, you know what I mean, there are attitudes remain in
one's mind for reasons that are clear, the carriage of a
head for example, bowed when one would have thought it
should be lifted, and vice versa, or a hand suspended in
mid-air, as if unowned. That kind of thing. But with your
father sitting on the rock that day nothing of the kind, no
detail you could put your finger on and say, How very
peculiar! No, I could never make it out. Perhaps, as I said,
just the great stillness of the whole body, as if all the
breath had left it. (*Pause.*) Is this rubbish a help to you,
Henry? (*Pause.*) I can try and go on a little if you wish.
(*Pause.*) No? (*Pause.*) Then I think I'll be getting back.

HENRY: Not yet! You needn't speak. Just listen. Not even. Be
with me. (*Pause.*) Ada! (*Pause. Louder.*) Ada! (*Pause.*)
Christ! (*Pause.*) Hooves! (*Pause. Louder.*) Hooves! (*Pause.*)
Christ! (*Long pause.*) Left soon afterwards, passed you on
the road, didn't see her, looking out to. . . . (*Pause.*) Can't
have been looking out to *sea*. (*Pause.*) Unless you had
gone round the other side. (*Pause.*) Had you gone round
the cliff side? (*Pause.*) Father! (*Pause.*) Must have I
suppose. (*Pause.*) Stands watching you a moment, then on
down path to tram, up on open top and sits down in
front. (*Pause.*) Sits down in front. (*Pause.*) Suddenly feels
uneasy and gets down again, conductor: 'Changed your
mind, Miss?', goes back up path, no sign of you. (*Pause.*)
Very unhappy and uneasy, hangs round a bit, not a soul
about, cold wind coming in off sea, goes back down path
and takes tram home. (*Pause.*) Takes tram home. (*Pause.*)
Christ! (*Pause.*) 'My dear Bolton. . . .' (*Pause.*) 'If it's an

injection you want, Bolton, let down your trousers and I'll
give you one, I have a panhysterectomy at nine,' meaning
of course the anaesthetic. (*Pause.*) Fire out, bitter cold,
white world, great trouble, not a sound. (*Pause.*) Bolton
starts playing with the curtain, no, hanging, difficult to
describe, draws it back, no, kind of gathers it towards him
and the moon comes flooding in, then lets it fall back,
heavy velvet affair, and pitch black in the room, then
towards him again, white, black, white, black, Holloway:
'Stop that for the love of God, Bolton, do you want to
finish me?' (*Pause.*) Black, white, black, white, maddening
thing. (*Pause.*) Then he suddenly strikes a match, Bolton
does, lights a candle, catches it up above his head, walks
over and looks Holloway full in the eye. (*Pause.*) Not a
word, just the look, the old blue eye, very glassy, lids worn
thin, lashes gone, whole thing swimming, and the candle
shaking over his head. (*Pause.*) Tears? (*Pause. Long laugh.*)
Good God no! (*Pause.*) Not a word, just the look, the old
blue eye, Holloway: 'If you want a shot say so and let me
get to hell out of here.' (*Pause.*) 'We've had this before,
Bolton, don't ask me to go through it again.' (*Pause.*)
Bolton: 'Please!' (*Pause.*) 'Please!' (*Pause.*) 'Please,
Holloway!' (*Pause.*) Candle shaking and guttering all over
the place, lower now, old arm tired, takes it in the other
hand and holds it high again, that's it, that was always it,
night, and the embers cold, and the glim shaking in your
old fist, saying, Please! Please! (*Pause.*) Begging. (*Pause.*)
Of the poor. (*Pause.*) Ada! (*Pause.*) Father! (*Pause.*) Christ!
(*Pause.*) Holds it high again, naughty world, fixes
Holloway, eyes drowned, won't ask again, just the look,
Holloway covers his face, not a sound, white world, bitter
cold, ghastly scene, old men, great trouble, no good.
(*Pause.*) No good. (*Pause.*) Christ! (*Pause. Shingle as he gets
up. He goes towards sea. Boots on shingle. He halts. Pause. Sea
a little louder.*) On. (*Pause. He moves on. Boots on shingle. He
halts at water's edge. Pause. Sea a little louder.*) Little book.

(*Pause.*) This evening. . . . (*Pause.*) Nothing this evening. (*Pause.*) Tomorrow . . . tomorrow . . . plumber at nine, then nothing. (*Pause. Puzzled.*) Plumber at nine? (*Pause.*) Ah yes, the waste. (*Pause.*) Words. (*Pause.*) Saturday . . . nothing. Sunday . . . Sunday . . . nothing all day. (*Pause.*) Nothing, all day nothing. (*Pause.*) All day all night nothing. (*Pause.*) Not a sound.

Sea.